STEP OUTSIDE

WALKING YOUR WAY TO HEALTH & HAPPINESS

STEP
OUTSIDE
PLUMLEAF PRESS

WALKING
YOUR WAY TO
HEALTH & HAPPINESS
BY LEE SCOTT

CONTENTS

“YOU ARE ON THE PATH TO A LONG LIFE FILLED WITH JOY AND EASE OF MOVEMENT.”
– LEE SCOTT

What
Matters Most
Is How Well You
Walk Through
The Fire

INTRODUCTION

"LIFE IN ALL ITS DIVERSITY UNFOLDS BEFORE US WHEN WE ARE ON FOOT."

~ JAN GEHL

THIS BOOK IS YOUR CALL TO WALKING.

I invite you to the outdoor gym — open to all. Get ready to embrace this place where your senses come alive with every step and equanimity infuses every cell in your body. As you open the door, trust that this book will be your guide to develop both the ease and the power that reside within you, whatever your age or ability. Your journey and your destination are contentment and good health.

SMALL WONDERS AND GREAT AWE ARE THERE FOR YOU TO DISCOVER BY SIMPLY MOVING YOUR OWN TWO FEET.

Perhaps because walking is something many of us are fortunate to be able to do easily, we underestimate its power to achieve remarkable happiness, health, and fitness. A walk can improve your mood within moments of stepping out your door — when you breathe in fresh air and take notice of the world outside. Walk a little farther and a little faster, and I promise you will find that the exhilaration exceeds what people typically expect from walking. When that walk becomes a daily ritual and you add mindful attention to the elements of gait, you are on the path to a long life filled with joy and ease of movement.

The daily walk ritual becomes a walk remedy with expansive benefits: profoundly connecting you with the awe so reliably manifest in the natural world, integrating you more tangibly with your community, making you physically stronger and mentally resilient, and giving you a sense of personal agency that is the secret ingredient for a satisfying life.

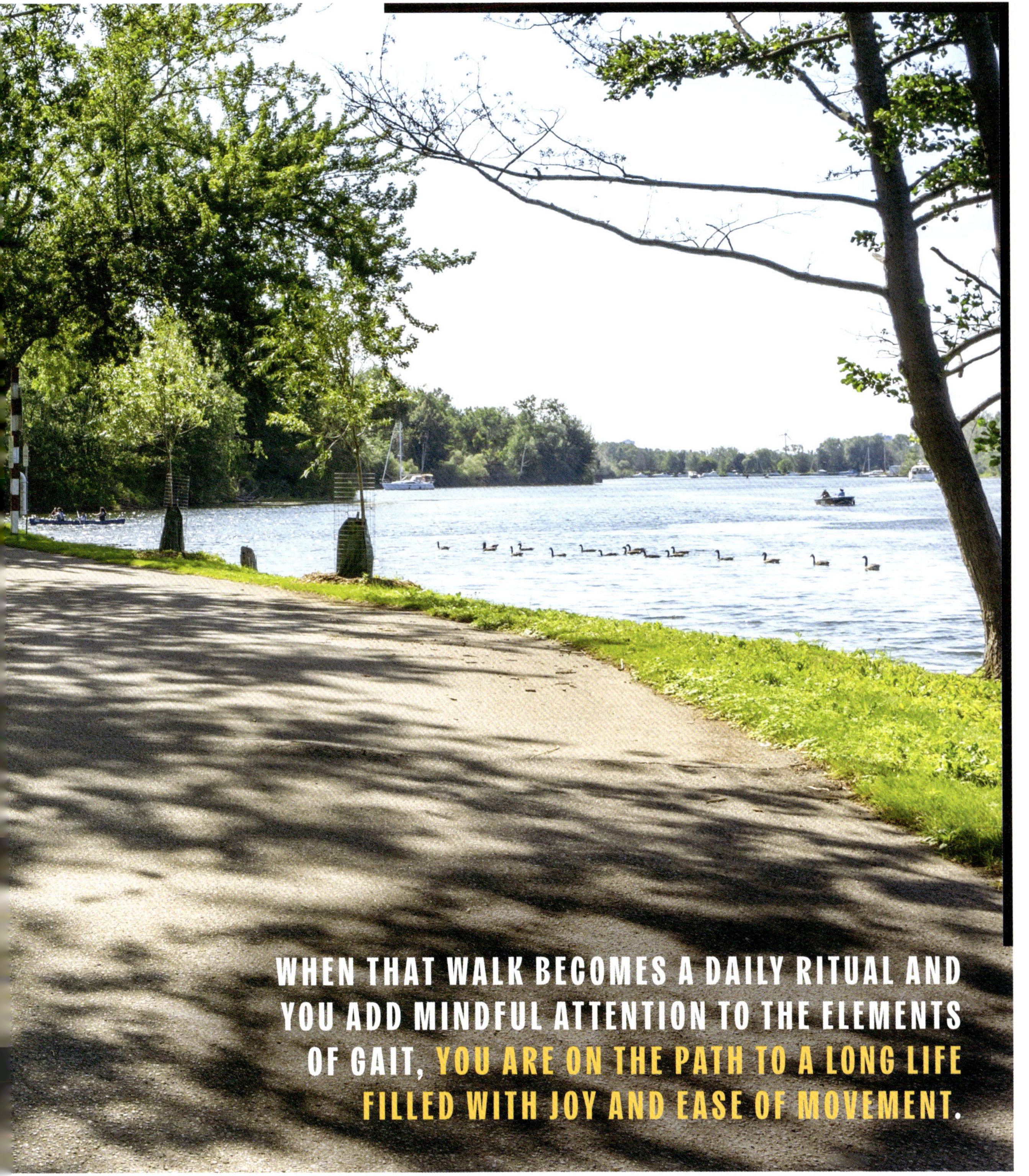

WHEN THAT WALK BECOMES A DAILY RITUAL AND YOU ADD MINDFUL ATTENTION TO THE ELEMENTS OF GAIT, YOU ARE ON THE PATH TO A LONG LIFE FILLED WITH JOY AND EASE OF MOVEMENT.

WALKING CAN TRANSFORM YOUR LIFE IN ALL THE WAYS THAT FANCY EXERCISE EQUIPMENT AND PROGRAMS PROMISE.

The fitness industry collects tens of billions of dollars in revenue each year, yet gym memberships go unused, fitness videos are abandoned, and hand weights are found at almost every garage sale. New Year's resolutions, forgotten by the first of February, are a testament to the challenge of staying committed to vigorous exercise. I encourage you to open the door and step outside for a walk.

Easy can get you out the door.

I love walking as exercise because it can start simply with an easy stroll. Over the years, many people have told me easy is not enough and asked me how to overcome the inertia of staying inside on the couch. Here's what I do — I remind myself to step outside with curiosity in my back pocket and with three guiding principles: I will feel renewed by fresh air within seconds. I can go easy if I feel like it. Outside is where I am most likely to find awe.

To see what is awesome, it is necessary to direct your attention outward and to connect with a detail or vista that expands your sense of the world beyond four walls and self-talk. It sounds simple, perhaps even glib. Yet I have found this inquisitive mindset works, and it's why walking has become my preferred exercise over anything I ever did at an indoor gym. I always take my phone on walks, using its camera to capture that unusual plant, a change in the light, or a novelty in my neighbourhood.

Each of my photos is probably better described as a momentary capture of a time when I experienced awe. These photos are glimmers — micro moments of awe. Sometimes glimmers are described as the opposite of triggers. While the human brain has a negativity bias thought to be important to ensure personal safety, we do recall moments of beauty and contentment. Many glimmers exist as moments we have experienced in nature: the glow of a sunrise or sunset, the sound of birdsong, the rich colour of a flower or garden, the chance sighting of a rainbow.

AWE CAN BE EXPERIENCED – AND GLIMMERS COMMITTED TO MEMORY – IN URBAN SETTINGS TOO.

Perhaps, as we are walking in the city, we chance upon an inviting bench, unexpected urban art, or unique architectural design. I have pulled out my camera for these moments too. The images in this book are a selection of glimmer moments, my library of awe, captured on camera while I was out walking.

It is possible to train our brain to seek out the glimmers. A camera is a fun way to record such moments. Even if I never look at the photo again, having taken a moment to frame the image in the lens, the glimmer has a permanent home in my memory. It remains like a seed growing into a desire to search for more. This is what I recommend as the starting point to creating your walk ritual. Build your glimmer albums and grow your awe library.

A simple outside walk can improve your mood. Adding vigour to that walk can lift those good feelings even higher and improve your cardiorespiratory health, your metabolism, your bone density, and your brain function. Every day, bringing some attention to how you walk can help you find the awe experience of flow and the contentment of mindfulness. If you can find contentment for some part of every day of your life, you are living an exceptional life.

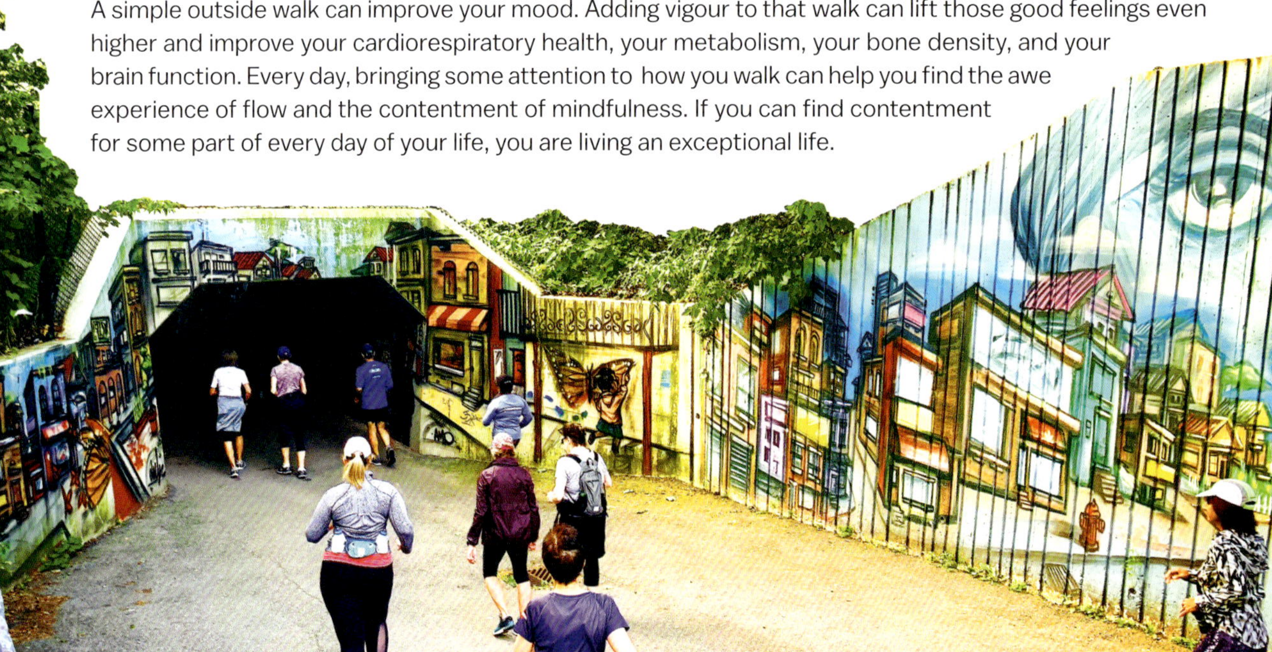

HOW TO GET AND STAY MOTIVATED

01. WRITE DOWN A SCHEDULED START TIME AND LENGTH OF YOUR WALK.

02. VISUALIZE YOURSELF 10 MINUTES INTO THE WALK WITH AN IMPROVED MOOD.

03. REMIND YOURSELF THAT YOUR HEART, YOUR BONES, AND YOUR BRAIN WILL ALL GET STRONGER.

04. WALK WITH A COLLEAGUE, FRIEND, OR FAMILY MEMBER.

05. VARY YOUR WALKING ROUTE – EXPLORE!

06. DRESS FOR SUCCESS – LOOK SHARP AND BE READY FOR ALL WEATHER.

07. USE A SMART WATCH TO TRACK YOUR SUCCESS.

08. LISTEN TO PODCASTS, AUDIOBOOKS, OR MUSIC WHILE WALKING.

09. COMBINE YOUR WALK WITH AN ERRAND.

10. GET OUT EVERY DAY – GIVE YOURSELF PERMISSION TO TURN BACK AFTER 10 MINUTES IF YOU NEED TO.

IF YOU CAN FIND CONTENTMENT FOR SOME PART OF EVERY DAY OF YOUR LIFE, **YOU ARE LIVING AN EXCEPTIONAL LIFE.**

SECTION 1

AWE

EXCHANGING MIRRORS FOR MAGIC

“EARTH’S CRAMMED WITH HEAVEN.”

~ ELIZABETH BARRETT BROWNING,
FROM “AURORA LEIGH”

MANY GOOD THINGS HAPPEN TO US WHEN WE STEP OUTSIDE, REGARDLESS OF THE WEATHER.

One feature common to almost all indoor workout space is the mirrored wall. Mirrors reflect and diffuse incoming light; they are installed to expand the sense of spaciousness and to provide an opportunity for participants to confirm that their body is accurately following the alignment cues given by instructors. However, mirrors can also invite comparison to others and result in a sense of low self-esteem.

Shifting to outdoor walks for exercise means leaving gym mirrors behind. This transition invites fresh air, sunlight, plants, animals, and, depending on where you live, sparkling water views. You can find beauty and joy. The experience is powerful because our focus shifts from judging ourselves in the gym mirror to engaging with the world surrounding us and with one another. When we walk with friends, we see their faces rather than our reflection. We may be absorbed in conversation or we may be simply walking side by side, but we unconsciously share a sense of wonder when walking together. Research on awe has shown that walking in unison can contribute to a feeling of "collective effervescence."

Reflect on an outside walk you have taken. Do any of the following emotions spring to mind when reflecting upon your feelings after your walk? Contentment? Exhilaration? Joy? Equanimity? Virtue? The simple act of stepping outside into fresh air can be life-changing.

IT IS POSSIBLE THAT SOMETIMES YOU DO NOT FEEL BETTER AFTER A WALK.

If that is the case, try to understand why. Are your shoes uncomfortable? Are you overdressed or underdressed? Did you feel unsafe? Could you be coming down with a cold? Have you been experiencing disrupted sleep? Did you eat too much or too much of the wrong food? Whatever the reason, ask yourself if there is a solution to this problem. What is one action you could take today to make your outdoor walk experience better? What about new shoes or different socks? Do you need more appropriate clothes to account for variable weather? Would timing your meals differently help? Would the kind of food you're eating make you feel better? Do you need to consider some different local routes? Do you need to check in with a health-care provider to rule out an underlying medical condition? Removing at least one of these barriers or taking one preparatory action moves you closer to getting outside every day and establishing your ritual.

CONSISTENCY IS THE GOAL TO WHICH WE ALL ASPIRE, AND YOU MAY BE SURPRISED THAT THIS IS MORE ABOUT MOVING YOUR MINDSET THAN YOUR BODY.

Even as a fitness coach, I am not immune to the contradictory and competing energies of modern life: the imperative of crossing off the next thing on my list and the comfort of my warm bed on a cold winter day. Most fitness, health, wellness, and lifestyle experts recommend creating a daily habit, or habits, to overcome these barriers. Many fitness specialists offer programs to help you build the daily habit. I support and encourage anything that will help you develop healthy lifestyle habits. I also encourage expanding your mindset.

Creating an active lifestyle

The transformational power of a daily walk outside requires replacing the idea of "habit" with "ritual." Where "habit" suggests simple repetition and consistency, "ritual" embodies a more expansive perspective, a routine that carries an almost spiritual meaning. In his book *Effortless: Make It Easier to Do What Matters Most*, author Greg McKeown describes a ritual as a "habit with a soul." He suggests reimagining our attitude and actions to embrace something we deem essential — in this case, creating an active lifestyle. What if, as McKeown suggests, we upend our perspective and reset our priorities, visualize how much it matters to us to be healthy, and believe this exercise and this connection with a world and community outside our own four walls will allow us to enjoy every day to its fullest?

The simple act of stepping outside into fresh air can be life-changing.

From challenge to commitment

You may have signed up for fitness challenges, such as "The 21-day strength challenge" or "The 30-day wellness challenge." This idea of challenge is typical of how we package the idea of getting exercise in a "should-do" wrapper that has hardship written all over it. We celebrate people who are "hard core" with their exercise: people who climb mountains over people who enjoy a quiet hike, people who downhill ski over people who cross-country ski, and people who run over people who "just walk." According to this messaging, not only should we exercise, but that exercise should also be *extreme*. It's as if exercise should be punishing to make a difference. All these messages of exercise as hard work are consistent with a belief system that glorifies pain and hardship as the only way to become strong.

But wait! What if we rewrite that script?

What if daily exercise is easy — or you can make it easy? What if exercise is something you eagerly anticipate and something to which you commit? What if we untether ourselves from a belief system that glorifies extreme challenge and attach ourselves to one that values ease, commitment, resilience, and contentment? When we honour ease, walking becomes a compelling and effective option for exercising. Here's the exciting twist: walking is not only an easy way to start, but it is also an easy way to keep moving, to add intensity, to become mindful of movement — all of which enhance health and well-being. When we take our walks outside, the mental health benefits of experiencing the awe available to us in the world may offer a singularly effective lifestyle tool to increase our health span — **a life that is not simply long in years, but also long in good health.**

COACH TIP »»

Schedule a minimum of 20 minutes for your walk. Visualize the first 5 to 10 minutes as easy walking and give yourself permission ahead of time to return home at the 10-minute mark if you do not feel your mood improving.

ANYONE NEED A LIFT?
MILE
14
Sponsored by
Lt. Col. Greg Mislick, USMC
Mind
Matter

SECTION 2

EXHILARATION

STEPPING OUTSIDE YOUR COMFORT ZONE

"TO ENGAGE OUR LONGEVITY GENES FULLY, INTENSITY DOES MATTER."

~ DR. DAVID A. SINCLAIR

EXERCISE IS ONE OF THE MOST EFFECTIVE WAYS TO ENJOY A LONG HEALTH SPAN.

From the moment you take your first walk, you are getting stronger. As you develop your walking routine, pay attention and you will notice that your energy for these walks is slowly but perceptibly increasing. At a cellular level, we have a miraculous ability to meet challenge with change — change that makes us stronger, faster, and more resilient. The adaptability and resilience of the human body — your body — can inspire awe in much the same way as what we see in the outside world. Get ready to exceed your own expectations.

In the 1950s, Hans Selye, who was then a researcher working at McGill University, developed a theory of stress response that is often referred to as the general adaptation syndrome (GAS). Selye, a renowned endocrinologist who was nominated for the Nobel Prize in medicine 19 times but never won, posited that stress — whether positive (eustress) or negative (distress) — led to adaptation in the body. Exercise is a form of eustress that leads to a positive adaptation in the body. Selye's theory continues to guide the principles of research into how the body gets stronger, faster, and more able to endure what it encounters.

MOVING TO A POINT OF BREATHLESSNESS IS CARDIORESPIRATORY EUSTRESS, AND IT HAS THE POTENTIAL TO CONTINUALLY IMPROVE PHYSICAL FITNESS.

Adapting to Increased Pace and Effort

Moving to a point of breathlessness is cardiorespiratory eustress, and it has the potential to continually improve physical fitness. Since the time of Selye's work, there has been an explosion of research on the benefits of the physical challenge we experience when exercising. These benefits of exercise accrue in virtually every physiological system and anatomical structure in the human body. We refer to these benefits broadly as fitness. The decades of fitness research continue to confirm that exercise is one of the most effective ways to enjoy a long health span. If you want to improve your fitness through walking, if you want to age well in both mind and body, you need to pick up the pace to a speed that offers good stress.

Two things will happen as you adapt to the eustress of increased pace and effort. First, you keep the same pace and finish your walk, having put in less effort than when you started walking, or you maintain the same effort level and complete the same route in a shorter time. You get faster for the same effort.

Walking with a faster pace aligns with public health recommendations to incorporate 150 minutes of vigorous activity into your week. Regardless of your current fitness level and your age, you can always walk fast enough that you get breathless and achieve vigorous effort.

How Do I Measure Effort?

Many fitness professionals suggest assessing your level of effort using a scale known as rate of perceived exertion (RPE), even though much of the fitness advice you will hear is about increasing your heart rate into target heart rate zones. Perceived exertion means how hard you feel your body is working. It is a rating from 0 to 10 given based on several factors you feel when you are moving, such as how fast your heart is beating, how fast and deep your breathing is, how much you're sweating, and how fatigued your muscles are.

It is important to trust how your body is feeling. Your chronological age, which is the basis for working in a target heart rate zone, is a number that may not reflect the lived experience of your body. All the components and systems in your body have aged in different ways, and the information they relay to your brain is complex. While your heart rate may be a good reflection of the composite picture, it is generally more accurate to assign a rating to how you perceive the effort of your walk pace.

If you own a wearable device (such as a watch or a ring) that measures heart rate, it may identify when you are working within the target heart rate zone for your age. Even with such a device, it can become a little obsessive to constantly check your device as you are walking. So, it is a good idea to become familiar with the cues related to rate of perceived exertion — particularly any shortness of breath that feels unmanageable. Listen to the cues.

Amazingly, **as you walk, it's not just your body that is getting stronger; your brain is changing too.** Simply stepping outside for fresh air and increasing your exposure to sunlight are thought to increase serotonin in the brain. Serotonin is a brain chemical, or neurotransmitter, that carries a message of well-being. You may notice your mood improves immediately from a little hit of oxygen and light. Certainly, after five to ten minutes of walking, the combination of an elevated heart rate and increased blood flow, along with fresh air and sunlight, will have serotonin sparking between synapses. I've noticed that any problem I was worried about before my walk was either resolved or determined to be manageable by the end of that walk.

The simple act of increasing effort in your walking results in significant improvements to most physiological systems in the body. Some of these improvements include increased cardiorespiratory capability, lowered blood pressure, increased neurogenesis (the making of new brain cells), improved metabolic function (which allows us to burn off more calories at rest), and improved sleep. Add to that the powerful effect exertion has on triggering the chemical messengers such as serotonin, noradrenaline, and dopamine, which make us feel good and powerful. This is the big win of walking fast — the sense of agency, mentioned in the introduction, is even more accessible when we step outside our comfort zone by increasing our effort.

WALKING AND RATE OF PERCEIVED EXERTION

RPE	EXPERIENCE	ZONE
1-2	Minimal to no effort	Zone 1
3-5	Stroll	Zone 1
5-6	Steady pace walk, body warming up, speaking easily	Zone 2
6-7	Steady pace walk, slight sweat, speaking full sentences, but attention to breath required	Zone 2
7-8	Longer (60+ sec.) interval pace, sweat accumulation, speaking short sentences	Zone 3
8-9	Shorter (<60 sec.) interval pace, more sweat, speaking one word at a time	Zone 4
10	Sprint intervals (<20 sec.), super sweaty, speaking is difficult, even impossible	Zone 5

It is important to trust how your body is feeling.

COACH TIP »»

Trust your recovery from breathlessness. If you find that you are having prolonged difficulty catching your breath (longer than two minutes), it's time to see your health-care provider.

Tapping into your inner athlete

You can purposefully invite awe into your walk ritual with attention to the exhilaration of exertion. In 2015, I was enjoying a delightful walking workout in wooded trails near my home. As I walked, I found the word "athlete" inserting itself into my thoughts like a mantra. It was probably no accident that I had returned just days prior from walking the New York City Marathon, where tens of thousands of competitors, from elite to amateur, make their way over 42.2 kilometres through the five boroughs of the city. Because there are upward of 50,000 people competing, the race organizers stagger the starts according to pace. We must wait in "corrals," and each corral is moved to the start line at a specific time. The year I did the race, the elite racers crossed the start line at 8:00 a.m. While waiting in my start corral, I excitedly watched giant video screens showing these elite runners assembled at the start line. They took off in a fine display of human magnificence — each one unquestionably an athlete. It was a moment of awe inspired by collective effervescence. I was a member of that collective.

As I walked in the woods that day, I found myself exhilarated by the flow of exertion and attention to my walking form. I felt a kinship with those elite competitors I had witnessed in New York City a week prior. As the mantra "athlete" reverberated in my head, I found myself asking what defines an athlete. The origin of the word is Greek and means "a contestant in games." Dictionaries may describe an athlete as "someone who competes in sports" or "a person who is trained in or good at sports." In my view, none of these definitions adequately captures the "spirit" of an athlete.

The spirit of an athlete is commitment. This spirit is effort and skill development. It is appreciation, love, and joy. The spirit of an athlete is dedication and discipline. It is respect and awe for the ability each of us has within us to exceed our own expectations. My life has been enriched by assuming the spirit of an athlete in my marathon preparation, but we can assume that mantle of an athlete without being competitors, in the way that I was an athlete alone in the woods that day.

Faster steps may be better than more

You can bring the spirit of an athlete into your heart and walk every day: exert yourself beyond your comfort zone and refine your walking gait to bring ease to that effort. That athlete's spirit will be more energizing than exhausting and more uplifting than arduous.

Counting steps — especially achieving a count of 10,000 steps every day — has become popular in recent years. I believe this focus on distance and the number of steps has distracted us from the value of speed. Counting your steps can be helpful if you are mostly sedentary and want to introduce some movement into your day. If achieving those 10,000 steps feels onerous, rest assured that you will feel more energized and improve your overall health if you simply increase the speed of whatever number of steps you are taking. The quality of those steps, not just the quantity, makes a big difference.

Picking up the pace of your steps from a stroll (rate of perceived exertion less than 5 on a scale of 1 to 10) to a power walk (rate of perceived exertion between 5 and 8) dramatically increases the physical benefit of those steps — including bone density. Bone is formed and strengthened by the mechanical load achieved during weight-bearing, postural, and balance exercises, and walking offers all three. Faster walkers typically experience greater impact force to their body upon heel strike than slower walkers or those who stroll. Although this impact felt by the fast walker is considerably less than that experienced by people running, it is sufficient to improve bone density.

The spirit of an athlete is dedication and discipline. It is respect and awe for the ability each of us has within us to exceed our own expectations.

During the Women's Health Initiative Observational Study conducted by the U.S. National Heart, Lung, and Blood Institute (NHLBI), researchers tracked the exercise habits of more than 75,000 women aged 50 to 79 for up to six years to see the effect of those habits on the prevention of cardiovascular disease.

Generally, women who walked 2.5 hours a week reduced their risk of experiencing a cardiac event such as a heart attack by as much as 30 percent.

A closer look at the details in this study reveals that greater protection against cardiac events comes with increased walking speed.

- Women who strolled between 2 and 3 mph [3.2 to 4.8 km/h] reduced their risk by 14 percent.
- Walkers averaging 3 to 4 mph [4.8 km/h to 6.4 km/h] cut their risk by 24 percent.
- Very fast walkers maintaining 4 mph [6.4 km/h] or more cut their risk by 42 percent.

Very fast walkers maintaining 4 mph [6.4 km/h] or more cut their risk of a cardiac event by 42 percent.

Fast walking also has benefits beyond cardiorespiratory fitness. The ongoing Nurses' Health Study into the risk factors for major chronic diseases in women found that women who walked at a brisk to very brisk pace experienced a 65 percent lower risk of hip fracture than those who were sedentary.

Increased walking speed can contribute to an extended life. Researchers at the University of Pennsylvania tracked approximately 5,000 older adults for an average of 13.5 years. The results published in 2014 show that those who walked at speeds faster than 100 steps per minute had a 21 percent reduction in all-cause mortality for the duration of the study. The reduction in risk increased as walking speed accelerated. For each increase in 10 steps per minute, an additional 4 percent reduction in all-cause mortality was realized. A pleasant surprise for many people is that the benefits of faster walking can be accrued over shorter walks. **It is often more manageable to set aside 20 minutes for a fast walk than 45 minutes for a slower walk.**

THERE ARE ADDITIONAL WAYS TO INCREASE THE EFFORT OF YOUR WALK OTHER THAN PICKING UP THE PACE.

Walk up a few hills or stairs! Hills provide natural strength training too. If you see a few stairs — or maybe even many stairs — on your walk, take them! According to the 2011 Compendium of Physical Activities, walking up an incline can increase caloric burn by about 60 percent without a change in speed from level ground, depending upon the grade of the hill. Even if you slow down as you climb, you may achieve as good a cardio workout as if you were walking briskly on level ground. Stair climbing has been measured to be twice as demanding as brisk walking on level terrain and 50 percent harder than walking up a steep incline or lifting weights, according to a Canadian study in the Department of Kinesiology at McMaster University. Slow and steady climbs can be just as effective as faster or higher inclines. **To protect the lower back from strain on both hills and stairs, maintain tall posture by looking up to where you are walking, lifting the rib cage, keeping a short stride length on hills, and sticking to one step at a time on stairs.**

When coaching a typical 60-to-90-minute walking class, we cover anywhere from 5 to 9 kilometres, and we always include speed drills and perhaps some hill-walking repeats and/or stair climbing to increase cardio eustress. Everyone has a different pace, but everyone gets breathless. These are high-quality steps. Class participants represent a range of ages from 40 to 80, so I know it can be done whatever your physical fitness, whatever your age, whatever your average walking pace. As a long-time coach, I have witnessed success, and I am confident you too can experience it.

COACH TIP ›››

Stretching after your walk workout is a good way to improve your performance. Focus on stretches that increase range of motion at the front of the shoulders and hips, and the back of the ankle. If you don't have time for stretching, that's fine; lack of stretching will not increase your risk of injury. Do ensure you enjoy a good five-minute strolling cool down.

HIGH INTENSITY INTERVAL TRAINING (HIIT) HAS BECOME ONE OF THE MOST POPULAR EXERCISE WORKOUTS IN RECENT YEARS.

Take a quick tour on YouTube for HIIT, and you may be surprised by what you find. It is common to see lean young people dripping bucket loads of sweat as they do things like a two-foot leap from the floor directly up onto high wood boxes — a workout for the already super-fit. The reality is that **HIIT is simply a description of a cardiorespiratory workout that alternates between movement at your perception of high intensity and movement at your perception of easy recovery periods.** HIIT is entirely aligned with your heart rate, your response to intensity, and your rate of perceived exertion. Walking can be a HIIT workout. It is possible to walk as fast as you can for short bursts and achieve a heart rate that is in your high intensity zone. **I call this WalkHIIT**, and it is as powerful for your health and resilience as HIIT workouts that call for greater impact.

Walking shorter distances at higher intensity brings big fitness and mood results for minimal time investment. Elevating the heart rate to over 7 out of 10 on the RPE scale brings exhilaration into a short 20-to-30-minute walk. After 10 minutes of easy walking to prepare the body for more intense movement, a few short intense bursts of speed fire up a physiological response that benefits the cardiorespiratory and metabolic systems while triggering a cascade of mood-enhancing brain chemicals — that's the exhilaration experience! For many people, this shorter time investment makes committing to the walk ritual easier.

You do not need to have a degree in exercise physiology or be an already fit person to WELCOME HIGH INTENSITY WALKING INTERVALS into your life. You can start this very moment with an informal HIIT walk that goes like this:

1. HEAD OUT YOUR DOOR AND STROLL FOR 5 TO 10 MINUTES.
2. CHOOSE AN OBJECT 50 TO 100 METRES AHEAD OF YOU.
3. WALK AS FAST YOU CAN TOWARD THAT OBJECT. (RPE BETWEEN 7 AND 9)
4. FOLLOW THIS WITH A SLOW WALK UNTIL YOU FEEL READY TO WALK FAST AGAIN FOR A SIMILAR DISTANCE.
5. REPEAT STEPS 2 TO 4 ABOVE, ALTERNATING SHORT, FAST SPURTS OF FAST WALKING WITH SLOW WALKING, 5 TO 10 TIMES OR FOR 5 TO 15 MINUTES.
6. STROLL HOME FOR 5 TO 10 MINUTES.

LONGER, LESS VIGOROUS WORKOUTS DO HAVE THEIR PLACE.

In Zone 2 workouts, your effort level is fuelled mostly by fat stores in your body and is measured by you as 5 to 6 out of 10 on a scale of perceived exertion. These workouts keep your heart strong and your metabolic system functioning well. At this level, you can talk easily while walking. Speaking from experience, it is the short walks that include some version of HIIT that improve my quality of life every day, and they are the walks in which I see clients improve their fitness most significantly.

In almost every walk workout class that I teach, I have a formula that I follow for introducing WalkHIIT. I coach two types of these intervals that I categorize as "go-recover" and "self-compete." During go-recover drills, there is a set time for walking as fast possible, alternating with a set time for easy walking to recover. For example, 5 intervals of 30 seconds of fast walking are alternated with 5 intervals of easy walking. It is my experience that people achieve a rate of perceived exertion in the range of 7 to 8 in these drills. When an element of self-competition is introduced, the effort level increases to 9 (almost 10). For example, during a self-compete drill, determine a set distance (perhaps 100 metres or one residential block). Walk that distance fast while timing yourself. Walk back slowly to your start position to recover. Then walk that distance fast again, trying to be faster than the first time. You can repeat this fast interval alternating with a recovery interval several times for a great workout.

"I COACH TWO TYPES OF THESE INTERVALS THAT I CATEGORIZE AS 'GO-RECOVER' AND 'SELF-COMPETE.' "

— LEE SCOTT

GO-RECOVER WALKHIIT

- SET TIME INTERVALS FOR A FAST WALK, THEN RECOVERY WALK.
- EXAMPLES: 5 SETS OF 30 SECONDS FAST WALK INTERVAL WITH 45 SECONDS RECOVERY (SLOWER) WALK INTERVAL OR 10 SETS OF 1-MINUTE FAST WALK INTERVAL WITH 2-MINUTE RECOVERY WALK. THE POSSIBILITIES ARE ENDLESS!
- RPE IS TYPICALLY 7 TO 8.

SELF-COMPETE WALKHIIT

- WALKING FAST TO IMPROVE THE TIME OF A SET DISTANCE OR THE DISTANCE OVER A SET TIME.
- EXAMPLES: SET A START POSITION. SET A TIME OF 30 SECONDS AND SEE HOW FAR YOU CAN WALK. REPEAT, TRYING TO WALK FARTHER. OR MARK OUT 100 M AND TRY TO WALK IT FASTER EACH TIME. (FOR BOTH OF THESE, YOUR RECOVERY IS THE WALK BACK TO YOUR STARTING POINT.)
- RPE OFTEN INCREASES TO 9 (ALMOST 10).

WHATEVER THE STARTING POINT IN YOUR FITNESS JOURNEY, YOU CAN EXPERIENCE THE EXHILARATION OF AN ELEVATED HEART RATE THROUGH FAST WALKING.

Work to *your* high intensity, to a level of exertion that feels like 8 to 9.5 on the 1 to 10 rate of perceived exertion scale, and you will improve your fitness. And yes, you can achieve high intensity cardiorespiratory exertion by walking your fastest. Today, you may feel that your exertion level is 8 out of 10 while walking at 2 km/h. In a few weeks, walking at that same exertion, you may discover you are walking 2.5 km/h; in a few months, that pace may be 3.5 km/h. Trust that when you invite intensity into your walk, at whatever speed that is for you, you will improve your health in ways that people typically associate with longer bouts of endurance exercise.

Ideally, include intervals in at least three of your weekly walks. These intervals could be included more often if you are giving yourself time to recover between workouts. If you feel genuinely fatigued ten minutes into any walk, you are probably working too hard or too often. That is a sure signal to take a rest. At the end of any walk, you should feel exhilarated by the challenge, not discouraged.

It is as much an art as a science to find a balance between progressing (that is, challenging your body to go farther and faster) and recovery (that is, the repair and building of muscles). Listen to your body, while remembering it has a predilection to conserve energy — which results in an affinity for the couch. When that affinity becomes too much of a good thing, return to the anticipation of beauty, and remember your heart is calling too. It wants you to fall in love with WalkHIIT!

COACH TIP »»

A reliable way to stay committed to your walk ritual is to make dates with a friend. When you make those dates, promise each other that one of your goals is to get fitter together. Dedicate a certain amount of time during each walk to a vigorous pace. For example, choose some of the Snap Walk Workouts found on pp. 64–67. Most of your walk will be spent at a pace that is comfortable for both of you to hold a conversation. When you introduce the vigorous drills, remind each other to take a break from the conversation, and encourage each other to walk at your fastest pace.

SECTION 3

PERFORMANCE

MAKING FASTER EASIER

"MANY OF THE THINGS WE FIND INTERESTING ARE NOT SO BY NATURE, BUT BECAUSE WE TOOK THE TROUBLE OF PAYING ATTENTION TO THEM."

~ MIHALY CSIKSZENTMIHALYI

MOVING FASTER WILL IMPROVE YOUR HEALTH AND FITNESS, AND BRING AN EXHILARATING SENSE OF AGENCY.

When you pay attention to **how** you walk, you can discover the miracle of mind and body working together to improve performance. Moving faster becomes easier, and you will exceed the health and fitness expectations commonly associated with walking. Bone density has been shown to be increased much more significantly with increased walking speed.

Refinements

To achieve greater speed, it will help to refine your gait. The **refinements** that follow will challenge your psychological comfort zone in a way that is different from physical exertion. We rarely, if ever, think about how we walk because our gait pattern is so well embedded in our body. And our gait is distinctive — consider how recognizable the gait of your friends and family members is from a distance. Have patience with yourself as you pay attention to changing your gait to be able to walk quickly for a low-impact workout.

After reviewing the progressive refinements and practising them, you may find that you enjoy using all of them together during your fitness walks, or you may enjoy spending a walk focused on one specific refinement. Trust your instincts about what feels good.

AS A COACH, I believe that focusing on easeful, progressive refinements to how you walk makes it possible to achieve the elements of flow as they have been described by psychologists:

1. Concentration on one action in the present moment.
2. The object of this concentration must be slightly out of your comfort zone.
3. Within the action, there are small, achievable goals.
4. As you concentrate on the action, immediate feedback is received.

All four of these flow elements are achievable by a walker at any fitness level or pace.

REFINEMENT 1.

POSTURE · STAND TALL AND LOOK TO WHERE YOU ARE GOING.

A strong walk begins with good posture.

Considerable research has shown that good posture can lead to health benefits, such as better balance, lower tension in shoulders and neck, reduced back pain and headaches, increased lung capacity, improved circulation and digestion, lowered wear on joints and vertebral elements, and improved core strength. Good posture even increases your energy as it decreases the strain on muscles and connective tissue brought on by misaligned loading throughout the body. Good posture helps you look and feel younger, and, importantly, moving your gaze up from the pavement connects you with the beauty of your surroundings.

1. Look to the horizon rather than to the ground. Understandably, we tend to look to the ground since we want to ensure that nothing is there to trip us up. The more you walk with your gaze ahead, the more you will become skilled at identifying hazards within your peripheral vision and calculating the time it takes to reach objects that require bypassing.
2. As you look toward the horizon, your ears will stack over your shoulders, which will stack over your hips, which will stack over your ankles. You will likely move faster from this simple repositioning of gaze and posture. Even if you keep the same pace, walking consistently with improved posture will encourage improved everyday functional posture.

Posture Matters!

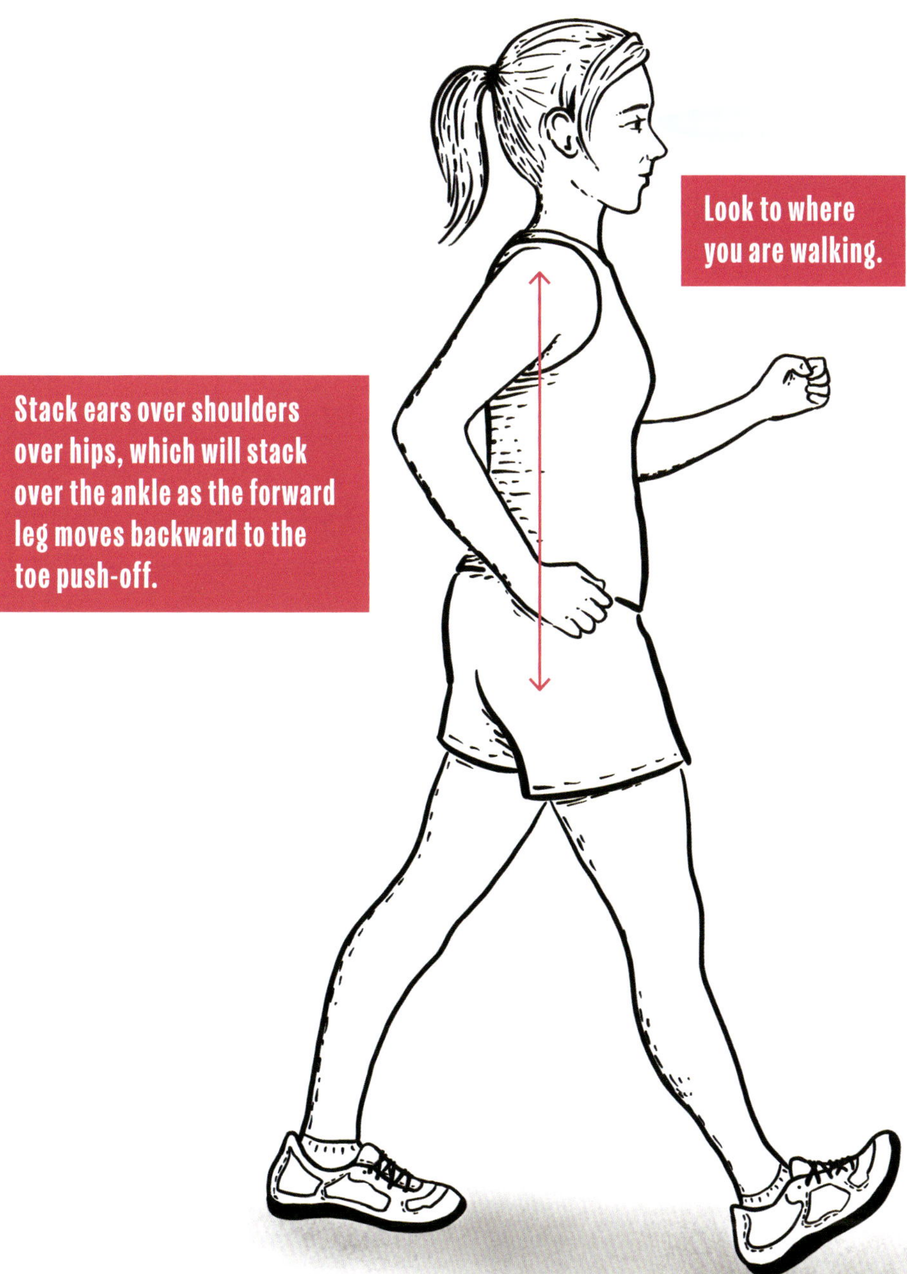

REFINEMENT 2.

ARM POSITION · BRING YOUR RUNNING ARMS ON YOUR WALK.

When good posture has been established, your arms can begin to work better for you.

1. Your brain knows instinctively that to run, your arms need to bend at the elbow. To walk faster, find your running arms by bending them at the elbow, and pump as you would when you run. Your hands should be in line with your forearms in a way that is relaxed without being limp and powerful without being clenched.
2. Once you get comfortable bending your arms at the elbows and pumping in this fashion, bring awareness to additional nuances of arm and hand position that will encourage ease and power:
   - Maintain alignment through the wrists so that your hands are in line with your forearm (i.e., hands do not hang limply).
   - Avoid clenching your hands into a fist (just a waste of energy!).
   - Limit arm movement upward so that your hands never punch toward the sky or result in a forward lean from the waist.
   - Limit excessive movement at the elbow.
   - Note the slight rotation of your arms toward the midline of your body because the shoulder is a ball-and-socket joint. Avoid excessive rotation of your arms around your torso so that your hands never cross the midline at the front of your body.

COACH TIP »»

Try to pull your hands back as far as the hip bone – even farther, if that feels comfortable. The farther you can pull your arm back, the farther back your opposite leg will move to give you more power from your toe push-off.

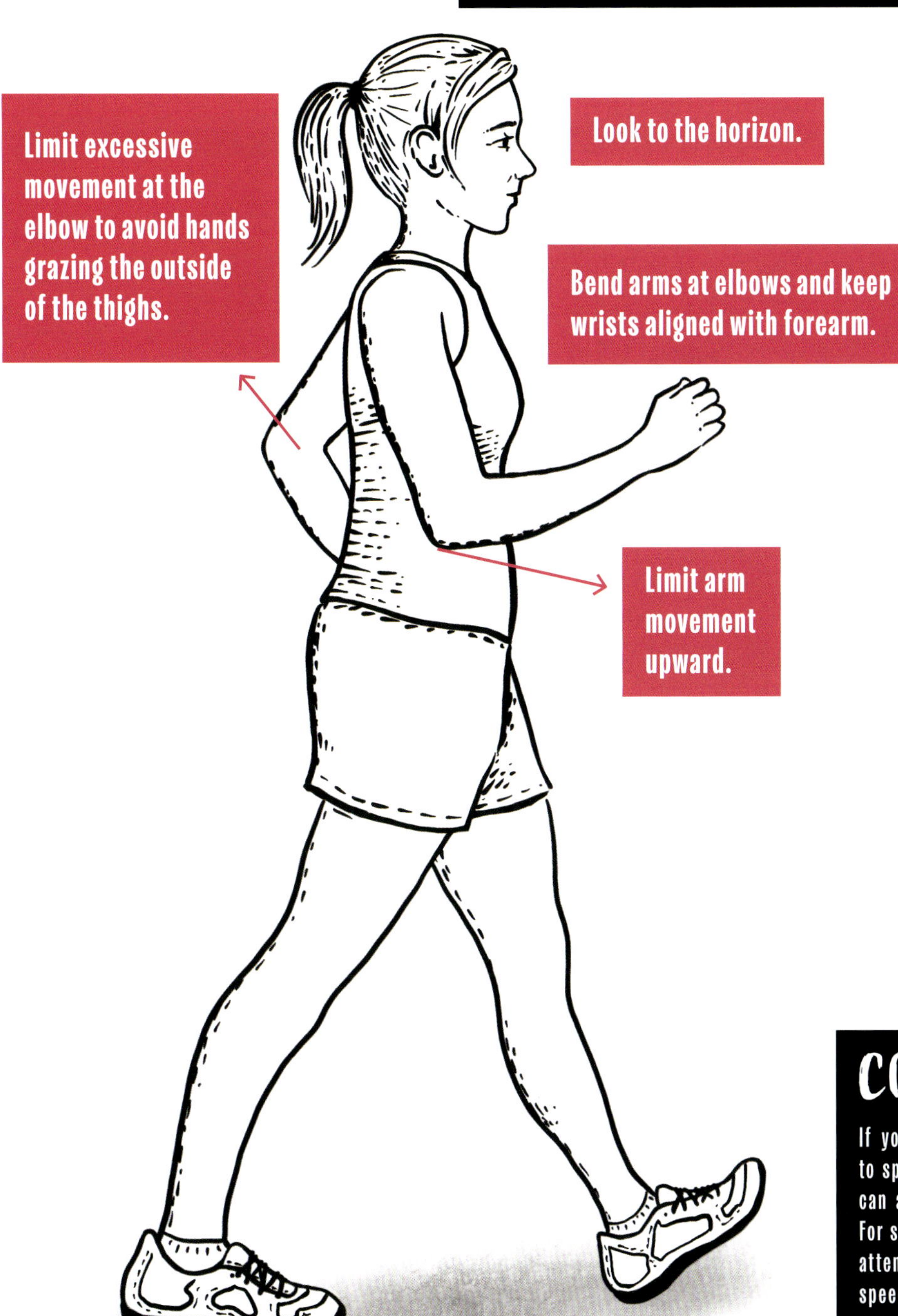

COACH TIP »»

If you want to get faster, you need to spend time walking as fast as you can and practising gait refinements. For some of your speed intervals, pay attention to the refinements; for other speed intervals, just go as fast as you can. Be in awe of your body. Trust that you will get faster with persistent effort and focus.

REFINEMENT 3.

FOOT POSITION · MAXIMIZE RANGE OF MOTION AT THE ANKLE.

Many people choose walking as a preferred form of exercise after experiencing injury to a knee joint because walking offers lower impact exercise than running and many other activities. It is usually assumed that simply lowering impact will help recovery, but good walking form can do even more to rehabilitate the knee joint.

1. A solid heel strike with toes pulled strongly toward the shin area and a fully extended knee joint as the front foot lands is your goal. In contrast, landing on a flat foot results in a flexed (bent) knee. An observer would identify that gait as a shuffle, or a slow jog, and the ligaments of the knee will continue to experience stress like that felt when running.
2. Pull your toes firmly up toward your shin to land on your heel and access the full range of motion at the ankle joint from heel strike to toe push-off. Also, achieving a solid heel strike when your foot touches the ground will encourage full extension of the knee on that front leg. This full extension lowers braking stress on the knee ligaments and distributes load up through the entire leg. This better weight-bearing load distribution can protect against knee injury while also improving, or maintaining, bone density.
3. The toe lift and heel strike of walking require contraction of the leg muscles alongside the shin. As you place more emphasis on the toe lift and heel strike, you may experience some fatigue or mild soreness in these muscles. Any soreness you feel should dissipate as you slow down and certainly several hours after your walk. If you find "shin fatigue" is distracting you during your walk, particularly during speed intervals, try walking backwards for several steps to release the tension. If you experience pain around the shin area that continues for hours or days after your walk is over, it is time to seek help from a health professional.

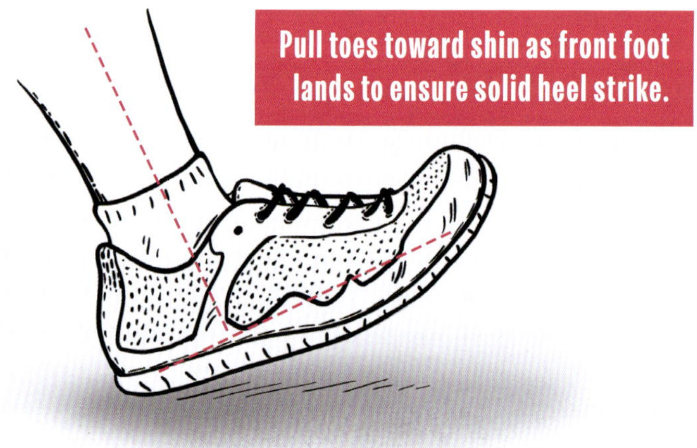

REFINEMENT 4.

STRIDE LENGTH · SHORTEN STEPS AND QUICKEN CADENCE.

Your stride length is a unique and consistent element of your gait signature. This fourth refinement to your walking technique increases the complexity of your gait and requires even more mindfulness than changes to posture and arm position. You may feel a frustration with this change because it may be more challenging to break a sweat than using your familiar stride length — this is particularly true if you are coming to walking from running.

1. Shortening your stride length means that the heel strike of your front foot lands much closer to your centre of gravity rather than ahead of it. This placement makes it easier for the back foot to push the weight of your torso over your front foot, minimizing the braking action of that front foot. The farther your foot lands in front of your body, the more it acts as a brake to your speed and the more it adds vertical motion, or "bounce," to your walk. You will know that you have shortened your stride length in front of your body sufficiently when you no longer notice any bounce to your walk.
2. As you walk with that shorter stride in front of your body, move your legs more quickly within the limit of that shortened stride. You are increasing the cadence, or pace, of your leg movement. If this seems tricky, try moving your arms more quickly. Whatever cadence you maintain in your arms, your legs will match. Also, you may notice that your shorter stride makes it easier to maintain good posture, and it may feel better for your lower back and knees.

Trust that this skill progression will bring you speed and sweat in good time, with lower risk of injury.

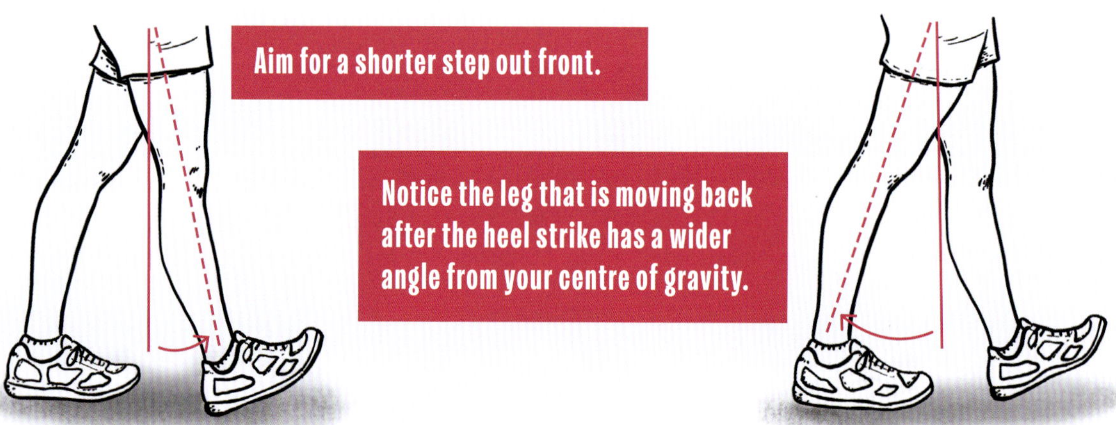

TRY IT IN PLACE!

LET'S TEST THE EXPERIENCE OF A SHORTER STRIDE.

1. Walk in such a way that your front foot is landing as far ahead as you can manage.
2. Take several steps with this long stride, and notice how your body is moving up and down as well as moving forward. This vertical motion is a waste of your energy and can increase the risk of injury over time.
3. Shorten the stride by bringing your front landing foot closer to your body. How short should the stride be out the front of your body? Just short enough to minimize the bounce.
4. The moment that you notice that vertical bounce is gone, you will have found your ideal stride length.

COACH TIP »»

Pain is your body's way of telling you something is wrong. Respect it. If the pain lessens as you ease effort, this means that your body is working to get stronger. Pain that does not resolve itself over the course of one to two weeks needs to be reviewed by a health-care provider. Your body always wants to heal; seek help if that is not happening.

REFINEMENT 5.

POWER BACK · USE MUSCLES IN THE BACK OF THE BODY TO MOVE FORWARD.

After incorporating positional changes in the upper and lower body, it's time to bring mindful attention to the strong muscles that will increase your speed, power, and workout. Most of these muscles are in the back of the body: the latissimus dorsi and rhomboid muscles across your upper back are larger than the pectoralis muscles of the chest; the gluteus maximus muscles (glutes) of your buttocks behind the hip joint are significantly larger than the hip flexor muscles at the front of the hip; and the calf muscles are much larger than those at the front of the lower leg. To shift focus from smaller front muscles to more powerful muscles in the back, we need to flip a switch in the brain. We need to THINK about initiating movement from the muscles in the arms, legs, and back.

1. Start with the arms. Their movement is usually easier to visualize than the legs. We have already established that to walk faster, you need to bend your arms at the elbows as you would when running. Now, focus on pulling your arms back, aiming to bring your hands back to the hip bone, as mentioned in Refinement 2.
2. Now, add the legs. Recruiting power from the muscles in the back of the front leg as it moves backwards after the heel strike can be a more challenging mental manoeuvre than intentionally pulling the arms back. We tend to focus on throwing the leading leg forward because there is little to resist the forward motion of that movement. Our brain follows the path of least resistance. We rarely think about the fact that after the heel strikes the ground, the glute muscles of the buttocks do some impressive work pulling that front landing leg behind us for the next toe push-off. Let's get the brain working to contract those glute muscles of the buttocks to pull the leg back!
3. Firing alternate glute muscles is tricky for the brain to coordinate, so try to practise simultaneously squeezing both glutes. This will power the leg that is moving back after the heel strike, while also shortening the forward reach of the leg after the toe push-off. As you learned earlier, this shortening of the stride length in front of the body is something you are trying to achieve to minimize vertical motion in your walk gait while maximizing speed.

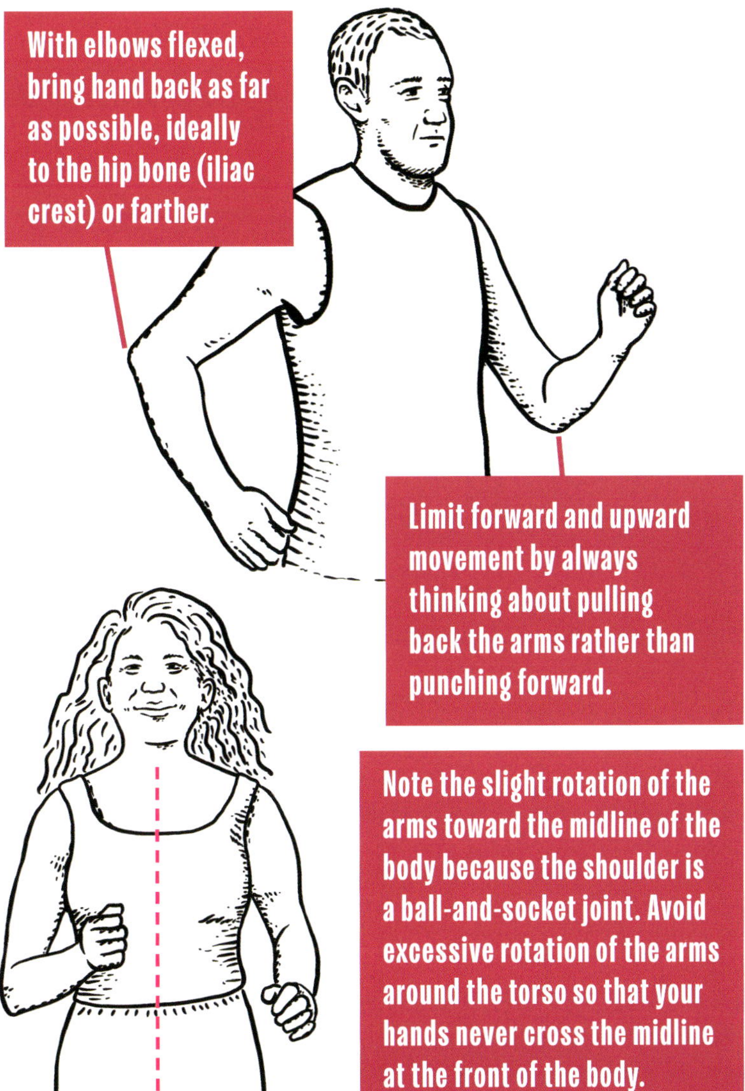

Bending your arms at the elbows makes the work through the shoulder joint easier, which minimizes the risk for overuse injury at the shoulder.

TRY IT IN PLACE!

IT'S WORTH DOING A LITTLE EXPERIMENT TO GET A SENSE OF JUST HOW POWERFUL YOUR ARMS CAN BE.

1. In a standing position, bend your arms. Imagine there is a punching bag in front of you. Moving your arms as you would when walking, visualize hitting that punching bag. Make a mental note of the power of that punch.
2. Now, flip a switch in your brain to initiate that movement in a different way. Visualize that the punching bag has moved behind you. Punch your elbows into the bag behind you.
3. It can help to imagine a place of power between the shoulder blades. As you pull back your arm, visualize contracting the muscles as if you are trying to pull your shoulder blades toward each other to assist with that backward movement of the arm (and to maintain strong upright posture).

Note the power you can achieve from your arm movement with this new brain emphasis. From now on, and as often as possible, think about pulling your arms back as you walk.

REFINEMENT 6.

RELAX THE HIPS/PELVIS · USE ABDOMINAL STRENGTH TO POWER YOUR WALK.

This final refinement may surprise you with the ease it can bring to your gait. It's a complex movement of the pelvis that resembles race walking, although it does not need to be as extreme in your body as what you can see in race-walking athletes. While race walking can look awkward to the uninitiated, there is much power and ease to be found from emulating elements of the style, especially relaxing through the hips and pelvis to allow what is commonly known as hip rotation. Prepare to find your groove to move your hips, increase your speed, strengthen your abdominal muscles, and expand your sense of flow.

Over my years of coaching, it has been common for people to come to me after I have introduced refinements 1 to 5 saying that they feel "robotic." **Such stiffness occurs when people increase speed without hip rotation.** It can feel like the powerful energy of leg movement comes to an abrupt halt at the hip. This halting can feel jarring and will certainly add an element of impact to your walk that may cause injury over time. If you have been experiencing this with your walk, implementing this refinement to find the groove of hip rotation should result in ease and speed simultaneously.

Although we tend to think of a race walker as someone swinging their hips from side to side, it may surprise you to notice that there is considerable movement forward and back, and this motion serves to power both legs and arms. **Pelvic rotation can be introduced to your technique by bringing awareness to two specific movements: foot placement and torso twist.**

1. Foot Placement. Placing your landing foot on the ground closer to the midline of your stride width is the easiest way to access movement at the hips and pelvis. Visualize a line on the floor directly beneath your navel, and bring your landing foot snug to that line without crossing it. Another way to visualize this new heel-strike placement is to imagine you are walking on a narrow plank that is just as wide as your two feet snug against each other.
2. Torso Twist. Actively using the abdominal muscles to power the movement of the pelvis (hips) is a second technique to access hip rotation. This movement requires a complex kinesthetic awareness. Foot placement along that imaginary narrow plank initiates the process. From that initiation, we must develop strong signalling between the brain and abdominal muscles to actively power from those muscles. If you can consciously bring mental attention to the contraction of your abdominal muscles to allow the movement of your hips forward and back, this muscle contraction will augment the effect of placing your landing foot closer to the midline underneath your body. The resulting torso twist, or hip rotation, will help you walk faster and intensify the workout while simultaneously reducing the jarring effect of referred impact at the hips.

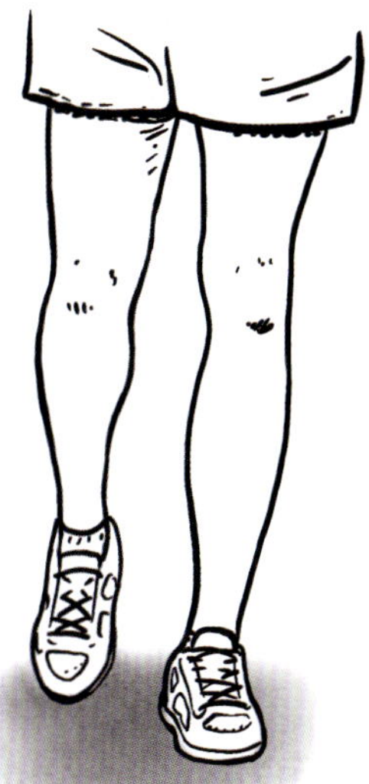

WIDE GAIT

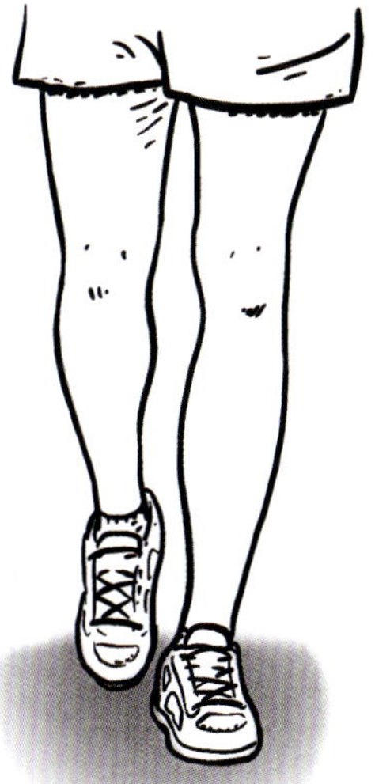

NARROW GAIT

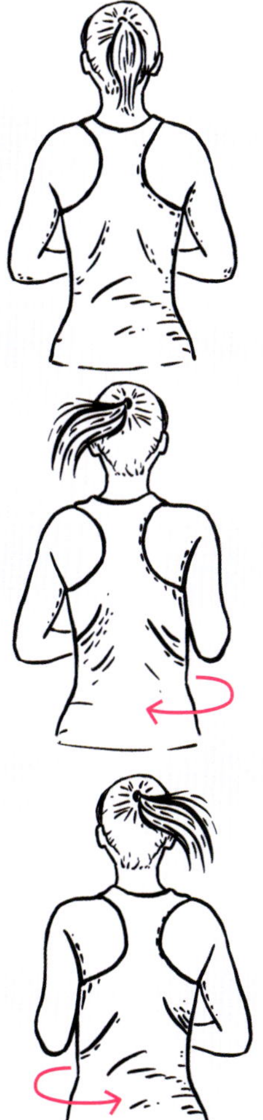

TRY IT IN PLACE!

NOTICE YOUR HIP AND PELVIS MOVEMENT.

1. Stand with your feet close together, and look to the horizon with your chin tucked back toward your neck.
2. Place the palms of your hands on the sides of your body between the bottom of your rib cage and your hip bone.
3. As you keep your upper body steady, especially your shoulders and collarbone, alternate bending each knee as you would while walking, keeping both feet planted on the floor.
4. Notice the movement in your hip and pelvis area, and try to feel the contraction of the abdominals that wrap around your waist contracting and releasing underneath your palms.
5. Bring mental attention to what you are feeling in the muscles surrounding your waist area. By consciously connecting with this muscle contraction, you may be able to recruit that muscle strength directly to activate hip rotation as you walk.

Bonus: this movement requires — and builds — powerful abdominal muscles.

Performance Review

Let's take a moment to go back to the beginning of our journey to refine walking gait, where we discussed simply starting with standing tall and bending your arms at the elbows. Bending your arms at the elbows is a guaranteed way to increase your walking speed. As you experiment with adding each of the refinements, you will find that your arms can work to your advantage even more. Everything is connected. Every muscle and connective tissue component surrounding your skeleton that can be recruited to move your pelvis and legs will support better and stronger movement in your arms. Furthermore, you will build strength in the back of your body that will enhance your posture. All these progressive refinements are amplified when working together to build a more powerful and mindful walk. There is awe in human performance!

COACH TIP »»

Key elements of gait refinement can be used as mindful focus points while walking.

1. Look to the horizon.
2. Bend arms at elbows.
3. Lift toes toward shins at heel strike.
4. Shorten distance between body and heel strike.
5. Pull arms back.
6. Squeeze glute muscles (buttocks) to get more power from the front leg that is moving back to toe push-off and to shorten the movement of forward-moving leg after toe push-off.
7. Bring heel strike closer toward midline of body (imagine walking a narrow plank).
8. Relax through hips and waist, allowing abdominal muscles to drive hip of returning leg.

SNAP WALK WORKOUTS

SNAP WALK WORKOUTS are fun and easy ways to add speed to your pace and vigour to your effort. The goal of the increased pace is to offer a healthy challenge to your cardiorespiratory system that will improve your overall fitness. These workouts can be introduced to your walking ritual three to five times a week. On other days, you could enjoy slower, longer walks or walk to do an errand.

Five to ten minutes of easy walking (strolling) should be included at the start and end of any Snap Walk Workout. This easy walking before the speed intervals prepares the body for more vigorous movement, and it may be one of the most important things you do to reduce the risk of injury. It gives the muscles and connective tissue time to warm up and prepare for the demands of greater loading.

Finishing each Snap Walk Workout with easy walking allows the heart rate to lower slowly. If you stop moving immediately after the vigour of speed intervals, you may experience a precipitous drop in blood return to the brain because the heart is still pumping blood vigorously to your extremities to deliver oxygen to the muscles of your arms and legs. If those muscles are not contracting because you are no longer walking, the blood pools in the lower legs and feet instead of returning to the heart and brain. This blood pooling can result in a feeling of light-headedness or even fainting.

Each Snap Walk Workout includes intervals of fast walking, known as a High Intensity Interval (HII), alternating with slower walking. The slower walking is known as an Active Recovery Interval (ARI), and it allows your heart rate to decrease and your breathing to become easier while keeping blood moving to the brain to prevent light-headedness. High Intensity Interval Training, such as these Snap Walk Workouts, is most comfortable 60 to 90 minutes after eating.

COACH TIP »»

Before stepping out for a walk you may want to pick one of the Snap Walk Workouts to boost results.

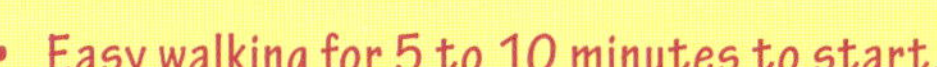

- Easy walking for 5 to 10 minutes to start.
- Identify a landmark from where you are standing and set a timer with an alarm for 10 minutes. From this landmark, walk quickly for 10 minutes until your alarm sounds.
- When your alarm sounds, turn around, set a timer, and walk as fast as you can back to your starting landmark.
- Have a look at your timer when you arrive back at your landmark, and note if you were able to walk faster on the return.
- Easy walking for 5 to 10 minutes to end.

- Find a walkable loop (residential block/parking lot, outdoor track).
- Easy walking for 5 to 10 minutes to start.
- Walk as fast as you can to a halfway point of that loop.
- Easy walk to complete the loop.
- Repeat 5 times.
- For a greater challenge, record the time it takes to complete each half loop. Try to decrease the time it takes to walk that half loop each of the 5 times.
- Easy walking for 5 to 10 minutes to end.

- Easy walking for 5 to 10 minutes to start.
- Walk fast 10 steps. Easy walk 10 steps.
- Walk fast 20 steps. Easy walk 20 steps.
- Add 10 steps to each fast-walking interval and 10 steps to each recovery walk interval until you have reached 100 steps.
- Easy walking for 5 to 10 minutes to end.

- Easy walking for 5 to 10 minutes to start.
- Walk as fast as you can for 20 seconds.
- Easy walk for 40 seconds.
- Repeat this interval sequence 10 times.
- Easy walking for 5 to 10 minutes to end.

- Easy walking for 5 to 10 minutes to start.
- Set a timer on your phone or watch for 15 seconds.
- Walk as fast as you can for 15 seconds, counting each step at heel strike.
- Easy walk for 45 seconds.
- Repeat the 15:45 interval 12 times (try to walk more steps in each 15-second interval).
- Easy walking for 5 to 10 minutes to end.

- Easy walking for 5 to 10 minutes to start.
- Mark a starting point at the bottom of a hill and a finishing point somewhere up the hill or at the top.
- Time yourself walking as fast as you can from start to finish.
- Easy walk to return from finish to start. Repeat 10 times.
- Easy walking for 5 to 10 minutes to end.

- Easy walking for 5 to 10 minutes to start.
- Start at the bottom of a hill. Set your alarm for ten 30-second intervals, with 60 seconds of recovery walking between each of those 30-second intervals.
- During the 30-second intervals, walk as fast as you can uphill while counting your steps.
- Walk downhill for the 60-second recovery walk.
- Each time you repeat the 30-second interval, try to move your legs more quickly with a shorter step to get more steps counted in that 30-second interval.
- Easy walking for 5 to 10 minutes to end.

- Easy walking for 5 to 10 minutes to start.
- Walk as fast as you can for 15 seconds, visualizing pulling your arms back.
- Easy walk for 45 seconds. Repeat 15:45, 6 times.
- Walk as fast as you can for 15 seconds, visualizing squeezing your glutes.
- Easy walk for 45 seconds. Repeat 15:45, 6 times.
- Easy walking for 5 to 10 minutes to end.

- Easy walking for 5 to 10 minutes to start.
- For one to two minutes of this easy walking, practise walking on a line or narrow plank.
- Then, walk at an easy pace for 15 minutes.
- Turn around to return home. Walk this return trip as fast as you can!
- Easy walking for 5 to 10 minutes to end.

- Write the numbers 8 to 12 on five individual pieces of paper. Fold each piece of paper, and put all five in a jar near your door. Pull one piece of paper from the jar. The number on the paper is the number of 30-second intervals of fast walking you will do after your easy walking warm-up.
- During these intervals, focus on looking to the horizon, with chin pulled back toward the neck, and arms bent at the elbow as you would do when you run.
- Easy walking for 5 to 10 minutes to start.
- Easy walk until you feel recovered between fast intervals.
- Easy walking for 5 to 10 minutes to end.

- Have a piece of chalk, or three small items (identifiable twig/leave).
- Easy walking for 5 to 10 minutes to start.
- Make a chalk mark or place an item as a marker for a start line.
- Set a timer with a noticeable sound alarm for 30 seconds.
- Walk as fast as you can for 30 seconds from that start point with one of your other markers in your hand or in a pocket. Place the second marker at this finish line, where your foot lands at the sound of the 30-second alarm.
- Easy walk back to your start point and repeat the fast walk (with the third marker), placing it at your finish line after 30 seconds. Pick up the marker that is closest to your start line identifier as you easy walk back there.
- Repeat from the same start line each time, walking as fast as you can for 30 seconds, trying to go farther each time and always leaving a marker if it is farther than the one left previously.
- Repeat until you are no longer increasing the distance between start and finish (or 10 repeats, whichever comes first).
- Easy walking for 5 to 10 minutes to end.

SECTION 4

EXPLORATION

AND IT'S ALL EXPLORATION

"TO WALK, YOU'RE SOME PLACE THAT IS ALREADY INTERESTING. YOU'RE NOT JUST BETWEEN PLACES. THINGS ARE HAPPENING."

~ REBECCA SOLNIT

I LIVE IN ONE OF THE MOST CULTURALLY DIVERSE CITIES IN THE WORLD.

Walking is powerful in its ability to improve health and fitness while simultaneously creating connection with the community and landscape. Toronto is a city where neighbourhoods are laid out like a quilt of ragged pattern and infinite colour. Over the 52 weeks of Covid 2020, I took a walk of 20 kilometres each week on different streets — 52 walks exploring my home. I saw random art installations, read words of encouragement for frontline workers artfully displayed in home and business windows, and took photos of rocks painted with whimsy laid beneath trees and along paths. I enjoyed trails cut deep into the land sequestered from the city above, where the only sounds were those of moving water and birdsong. I smelled the fragrance of the food created by people from all over the world who now make Toronto their home — Jamaican patties, Indian curries and grilled naan, Vietnamese pho, French croissants, Korean barbecue, sourdough breads, and much more. I saw individuals, couples, families, and friends walking Toronto streets, trails, and parks. My profound learning from the year-long odyssey was that the excitement of exploration is possible just outside my front door, in my own neighbourhood and city, at any time.

WALKING IS POWERFUL IN ITS ABILITY TO IMPROVE HEALTH AND FITNESS WHILE SIMULTANEOUSLY CREATING CONNECTION WITH THE COMMUNITY AND LANDSCAPE.

CONSIDER EXPLORATION THAT ASKS YOU TO STEP OUTSIDE YOUR COMFORT ZONE – BOTH PHYSICALLY AND MENTALLY.

Exploration can take place farther from home. If you have experienced the joy of physical exertion — the joy of getting sweaty while walking — you know that challenge can be experienced without misery. Why not take exertion and exhilaration to the next level and register to walk in a race?

FAST: WALK IN A RACE

Many people think that road races are just for runners, yet nearly all races can be walked. For more than 20 years, I have been coaching people to walk in competitive races, and I have walked hundreds myself — races of varying distances including 5k, 10k, half-marathons (21.1k), marathons (42.2k), and even ultramarathons (anything longer than 42.2k). Race organizers often welcome walkers. This welcome generally translates into extended time limits for completion. Typically, but not always, people who walk will need more time to complete any distance than those who are running.

Sometimes, races offer designated walk divisions. Competitors must use only the walking gait for the duration of the race. Without such a designated division, walkers are ranked against runners as they are in most races. Organizers who offer walk divisions are rare, so their efforts are greatly appreciated. A walk division levels the playing field, giving walkers the unique experience of competing against people using the same gait rather than those advantaged by the runners' spring action of a bent knee in the front landing leg.

Most races feature a charity component, and this is motivation for many people to register. Look for races in your own town or region that may raise money for a local charity. Participating in these races as both a competitor and a fundraiser is a great way to get outside, complete a fitness goal, and support your community. If you think that registering for a race would be a goal that motivates you to be active, preparing a training schedule of three to five walking workouts each week will set you up for success. Some of these workouts should include speed interval training, and one walk a week should slowly increase the distance to approach the distance you will be required to walk on race day. Endurance walks, together with the speed workouts, set you up for success to complete the race within the time limit.

Participating in a race offers a profound experience of moving together. After gathering in unison waiting for the starting gun to sound, racers of all shapes and sizes forge ahead. There is a moment of shared exhilaration and awe from the communal movement and human connection. Everyone at that start line knows what it took to get to that place. There may be other opportunities after the start and during the race when you might see a vista of hundreds, or thousands, or even tens of thousands of fellow humans all moving together toward the finish line. It's rare in the sports world to be able to participate in an event that allows so many people of such varying skill levels to participate at the same time. As a walker, you can be an essential ingredient in the creation of a collective effervescence experience.

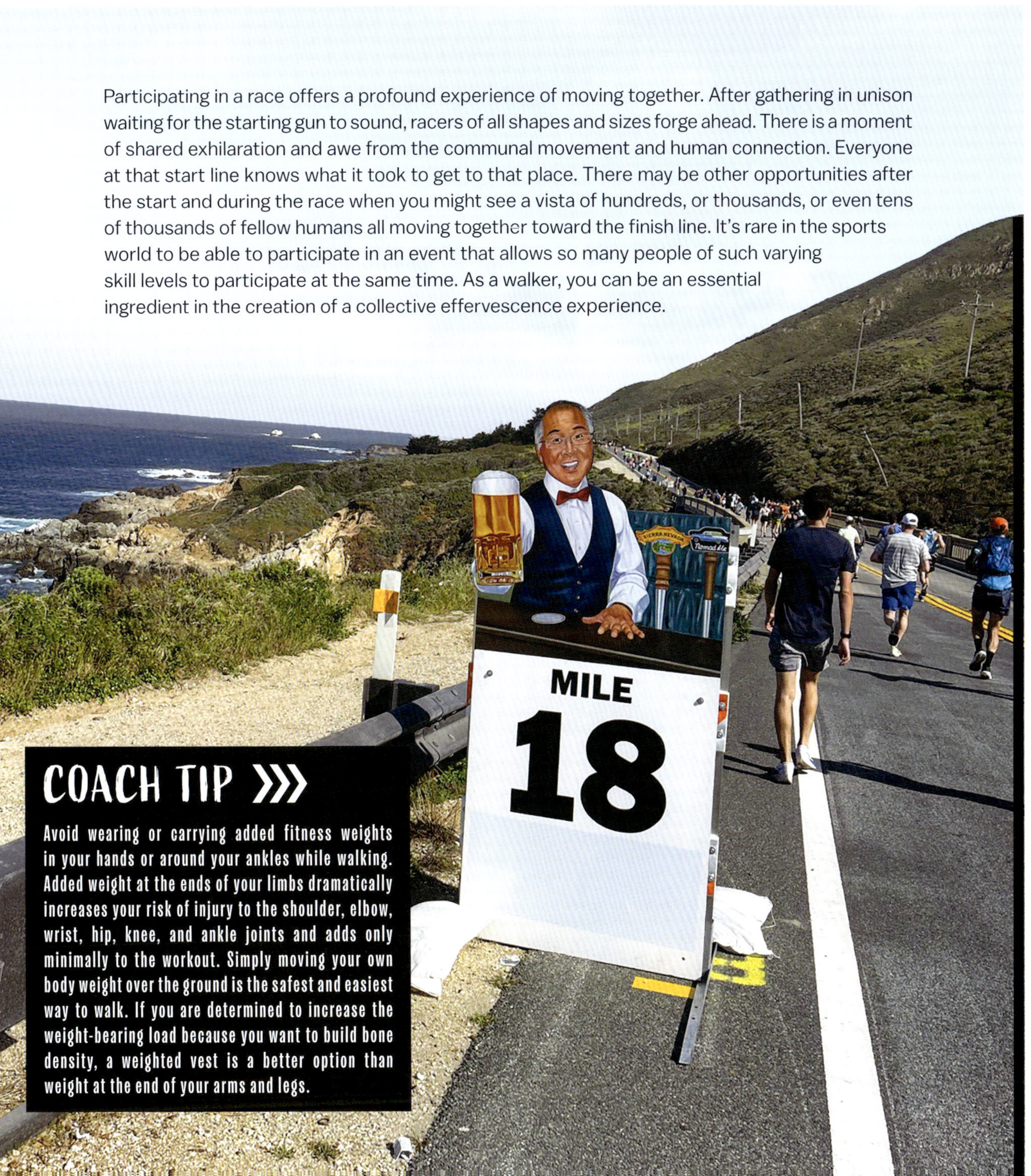

COACH TIP »»

Avoid wearing or carrying added fitness weights in your hands or around your ankles while walking. Added weight at the ends of your limbs dramatically increases your risk of injury to the shoulder, elbow, wrist, hip, knee, and ankle joints and adds only minimally to the workout. Simply moving your own body weight over the ground is the safest and easiest way to walk. If you are determined to increase the weight-bearing load because you want to build bone density, a weighted vest is a better option than weight at the end of your arms and legs.

SLOW: HOLIDAY RAMBLE

Much different from local exploration or racing is the setting of travel goals that involve walking. In 2016, I walked the length of Hadrian's Wall Path in northern England at the pace of a slow stroll. The wall was built for the Roman emperor Hadrian to offer defence from northern invaders. The invasion never happened, but remnants of the wall, turrets, and settlements remain. It turns out Hadrian built a route with guideposts for people to walk across the route 2,000 years in the future. It was the best holiday. For eight to ten hours every day, my partner and I rambled in companionable silence, frequently stopping to read the guidebook. We took an embarrassing number of photos of sheep and cows, sat on rocks or under trees for short picnics, and once happened upon a pub featuring a roaring fire shortly after walking through a massive rainstorm. We detoured for the best tea and scones, and every day we would finish at a local pub with a robust meal and a beer or a whisky. We slept soundly. Once you become accustomed to a life abundant in daily walking, you may find you want your vacations to emulate a similar experience on a slightly grander scale. You begin to exceed your expectations of what is possible.

Even holiday plans that are not designed specifically around walking can be revised to incorporate it. If you find yourself going to a hotel gym, ask yourself if you could instead walk in the neighbourhood where the hotel is located. In 2009, I attended a conference in Richmond, British Columbia. Richmond struck me as rather overwhelmingly concrete, so I decided to simply do a walk workout on the treadmill in the hotel gym. As I began the walk in the tiny airless room watching multiple screens broadcasting more bad news, I gave my head a shake. I figured the opportunity to breathe fresh air had to be an improvement on my current situation. I got off the treadmill and stepped outside to walk. Within 15 minutes, I had happened upon what I thought was a beautiful new community centre, and I went inside. I had stumbled upon what was to be the short-track speed skating venue for the Vancouver 2010 Olympics. The building was stunning. Bigger than six football fields, its soaring open span ceiling was constructed using wood salvaged from forests felled by pine beetles. That is a walk I shall always remember.

Fully recognizing that there are places where walking may not be viable for a host of reasons — too hot, too icy, poor pedestrian infrastructure, dangerous animals — taking a walk outside a hotel, rather than inside, offers the possibility of surprise and delight and is my preference. On those occasions when I have resorted to a treadmill, I take the "glass half-full" mindset, appreciating the opportunity to feel the exhilaration of exertion as I conduct the same high intensity walk drills I would do outside but on the treadmill. Additionally, the ability to control speed and incline on a treadmill can be helpful for practising effective walking form under steady conditions. All forms work to connect me to the awe of flow and mindfulness.

COACH TIP »»

Not knowing where there is public access to a washroom can be a barrier to taking outdoor walks when you are in an unfamiliar place. Many app-based maps will offer suggestions if you type in "public restroom." Also, it's a good idea to carry extra tissue and hand sanitizer.

WE ENCOURAGE THE EXPLORER MINDSET WITH EVERY WALK.

The quality of your life, including your mental and physical health, benefits from the outdoor walk experience when you actively pursue awe, exhilaration, and ease. This explorer mindset moves us away from associating walking with the word "just." There's no *just* walking. Our bipedal experience is unique to humans. We honour that uniqueness when we step outside with a sense of ritual and an eye for awe, an invitation for vigour with ease, and always a curious disposition.

TO PARAPHRASE THE OPENING QUOTE OF THIS SECTION FROM REBECCA SOLNIT: STEP OUTSIDE AND YOU ARE SOMEWHERE ...

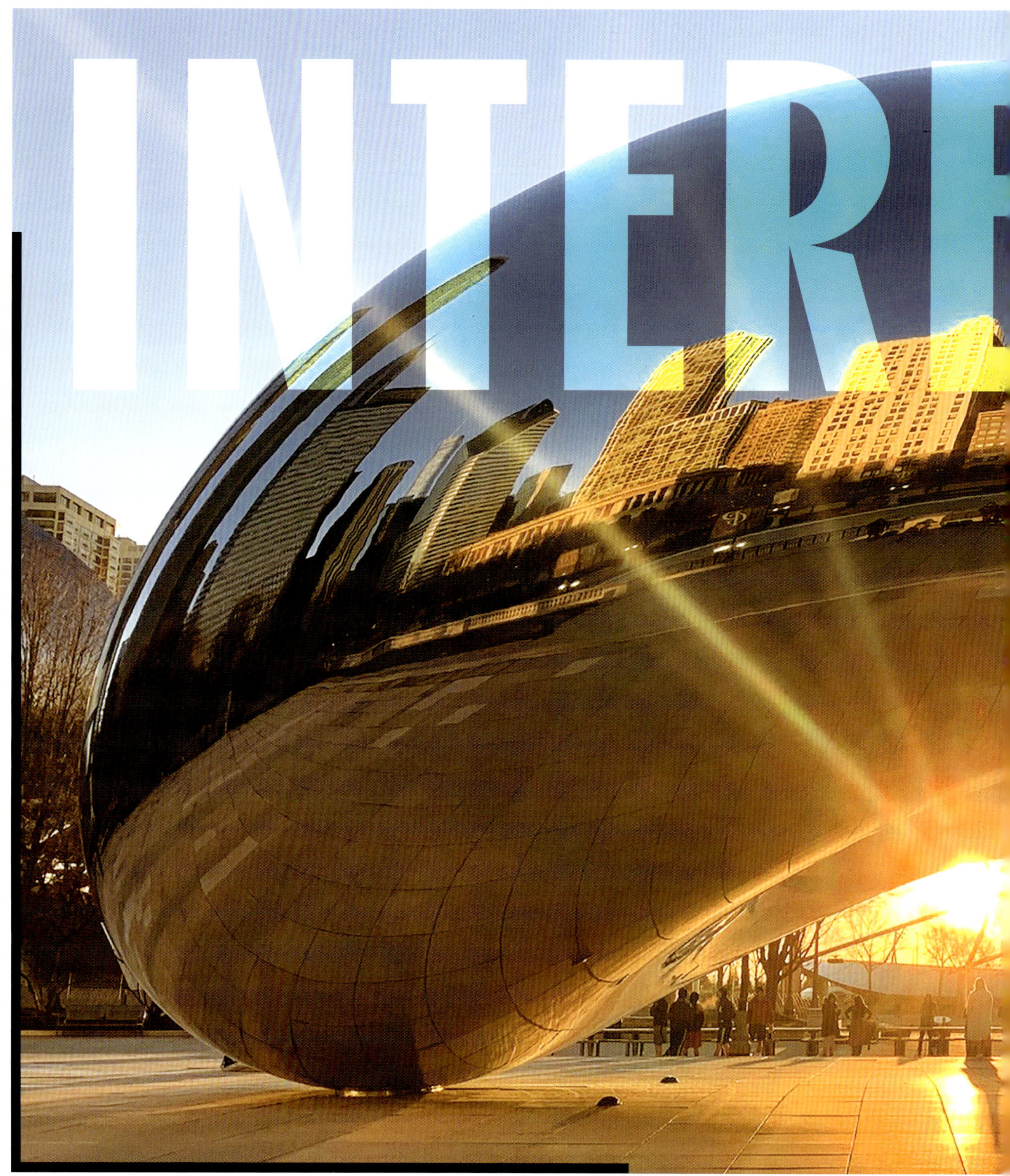
INTER

STING

ENERG

IZING

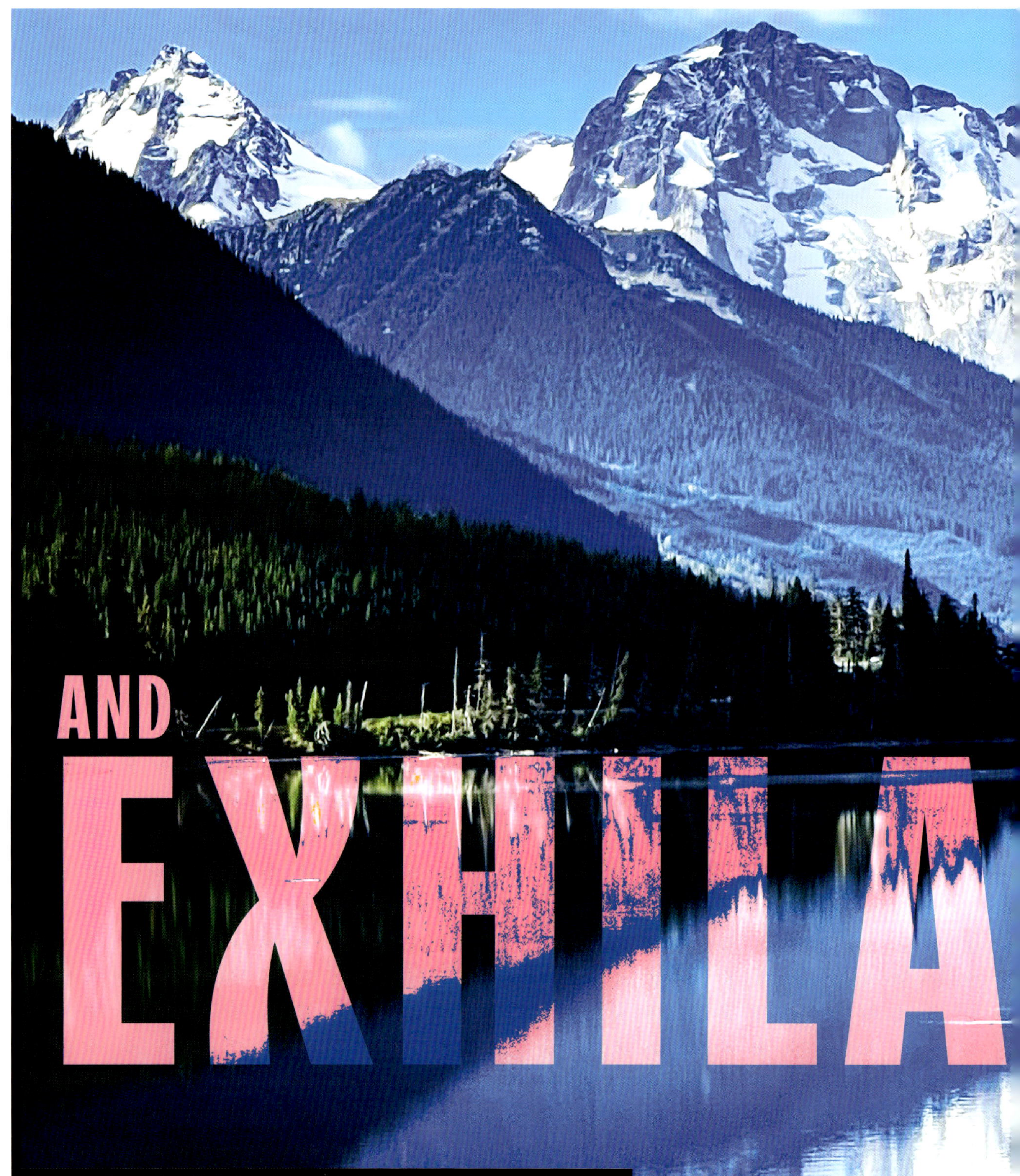
AND
EXHILA

RATING.
~ LEE SCOTT

REFERENCES AND FURTHER READING

SECTION 1: AWE – Exchanging Mirrors for Magic

Barton, J. & Pretty, J. (2010). What is the best dose of nature and green exercise for improving mental health? A multi-study analysis. *Environmental Science & Technology, 44*(10), 3947–3955. https://doi.org/10.1021/es903183r.

Blume, C., Garbazza, C. & Spitschan, M. Effects of light on human circadian rhythms, sleep and mood. (2019). *Somnologie, 23*(3), 147–156. doi: 10.1007/s11818-019-00215-x.

Dana, Deb. (2018). *The polyvagal theory in therapy: Engaging the rhythm of regulation.* New York: W. W. Norton & Company.

Keltner, Dacher. (2023). *Awe: The new science of everyday wonder and how it can transform your life*. New York: Penguin Random House.

Kühn, S., Mascherek, A., Filevich, E., Lisofsky, N., Becker, M., Butler, O., Lochstet, M., Mårtensson, J., Wenger, E., Lindenberger, U. & Gallinat, J. (2022). Spend time outdoors for your brain – an in-depth longitudinal MRI study. *The World Journal of Biological Psychiatry, 23*(3), 201–207. doi: 10.1080/15622975.2021.1938670.

Williams, F. (2017). *The nature fix: Why nature makes us happier, healthier, and more creative*. New York: W. W. Norton & Company.

SECTION 2: EXHILARATION – Stepping Out of Your Comfort Zone

Attia, Peter. (2023). *Outlive: The science & art of longevity*. New York: Harmony Books.

Benn, S. J., McCartney, N., & McKelvie, R.S. (1996). Circulatory responses to weightlifting, walking, and stair climbing in older males. *Journal of the American Geriatrics Society, 44*(2), 121–125. doi: 10.1111/j.1532-5415.1996.tb02426.x.

Brown, J. C. , Harhay, M. O. & Harhay, M. N. (2024). Walking cadence and mortality among community-dwelling older adults. *Journal of General Internal Medicine, (29)*9, 1263–1269. https://doi.org/10.1007/s11606-014-2926-6.

The Canadian Society for Exercise Physiology (CSEP). *24-Hour Movement Guidelines.* Retrieved from https://csepguidelines.ca/.

Centers for Disease Control and Prevention. *Move Your Way: What's your move?* Retrieved from https://health.gov/sites/default/files/2019-11/PAG_MYW_Adult_FS.pdf.

Gibala, M. (2017). *The one-minute workout: Science shows a way to get fit that's smarter, faster, shorter*. New York: Penguin Random House.

Kimiecik, Jay C. (2002). *The intrinsic exerciser: Discovering the joy of exercise*. Boston: Houghton Mifflin Harcourt.

Mandsager, K., Harb, S., Cremer, P., Phelan, D., Nissen S. E., & Jaber, W. Association of cardiorespiratory fitness with long-term mortality among adults undergoing exercise treadmill testing. (2018). *JAMA Network Open, 1*(6), doi:10.1001/jamanetworkopen.2018.3605.

Middleton, A., Fritz, S.L., & Lusardi, M. (2015). Walking speed: The functional vital sign. *Journal of Aging and Physical Activity, 23*(2), 314–322.

Momma, H., Kawakami, R., Honda, T., & Sawada, Susumu S. (2022). Muscle-strengthening activities are associated with lower risk and mortality in major non-communicable diseases: a systematic review and meta-analysis of cohort studies. *British Journal of Sports Medicine, 56*(13): 755–763. doi: 10.1136/bjsports-2021-105061.

National Heart, Lung and Blood Institute. (2012). *Women's Health Initiative: Clinical Trial and Observational Study (WHI-CTOS)*. Retrieved from https://www.whi.org/papers.

National Library of Medicine. (2011). 2011 *Compendium of Physical Activities: a second update of codes and MET values*. Retrieved from https://pubmed.ncbi.nlm.nih.gov/21681120/.

Nurses' Health Study. Retrieved from https://nurseshealthstudy.org.

Robinson, M. M., Dasari, S., Konopka, A. R., Johnson, M. L., Manjunatha, S., Esponda, R. R., Carter, R. E., Lanza, I. R., & Sreekumaran Nair, K. (2017). Enhanced protein translation underlies improved metabolic and physical adaptations to different exercise training modes in young and old humans. *Cell Metabolism, 25*(3),581–592. doi: 10.1016/j.cmet.2017.02.009.

Selye, H. (1950). Stress and the general adaptation syndrome. *British Medical Journal, 1*(1383), 1383–1392. https://doi.org/10.1136/bmj.1.4667.1383.

Sims, Stacy T. & Yeager, S. (2022) *Next level: Your guide to kicking ass, feeling great, and crushing goals through menopause and beyond.* New York: Rodale Books, an Imprint of Random House.

Sims, Stacy T. & Yeager, S. (2024) *Roar: Match your food and fitness to your unique female physiology for optimum performance, great health, and a strong body for life.* New York: Rodale Books, an Imprint of Random House.

Sturm, V. E., Datta, S., Roy, A.R.K., Sible, I. J., Kosik, E. L., Veziris, C. R., Chow, T. E., Morris, N. A., Neuhaus, J., Kramer, J. H., Miller, B. L., Holley, S. R., & Keltner, D. (2022). Big smile, small self: Awe walks promote prosocial positive emotions in older adults. *Emotion, 22*(5), 1044–1058. https://doi.org/10.1037/emo0000876.

Tudor-Locke, C., Han, H., Aguiar, E. J., Barreira, T. V., Schuna, J. M. Jr., Kang, M., & Rowe, D. A. (2018). How fast is fast enough? Walking cadence (steps/min) as a practical estimate of intensity in adults: a narrative review. *British Journal of Sports Medicine, 52*(12), 776–788.

World Health Organization. (2022). *Physical Activity*. Retrieved from https://www.who.int/news-room/fact-sheets/detail/physical-activity.

Zinoubi, B., Zbidi, S., Vandewalle, H., Chamari, K., & Driss, T. (2018). Relationships between rating of perceived exertion, heart rate and blood lactate during continuous and alternated-intensity cycling exercises. *Biology of Sport, 35*(1), 29–37. doi:10.5114/biolsport.2018.70749.

SECTION 3: PERFORMANCE – Making Faster Easier

Chiricoa, A., & Gaggioli, A. (2018). The continuum of self-transcendence: Flow experience and the emotion of awe. *Annual Review of CyberTherapy and Telemedicine, 16*, 67–72.

Csikszentmihalyi, M. (1990). *Flow: The psychology of optimal experience*. New York: Harper and Row.

Earls, J. (2020). *Born to walk: Myofascial efficiency and the body in movement* (2nd ed.). Chichester, West Sussex: Lotus Publishing.

Iknoian, T. (1998). *Walking fast: Techniques and workouts for high-level fitness and performance*. Champaign, IL: Human Kinetics.

Kim, Y., Nusbaum, H. C., & Yang, F. (2022). Going beyond ourselves: The role of self-transcendent experiences in wisdom. *Cognition and Emotion, 37*(1), 98–116.1–19. doi:10.1080/02699931.2022.2149473.

McGill, Stuart. (2017). *Back Mechanic: The secrets to a healthy spine your doctor isn't telling you*. Gravenhurst, ON: Backfitpro Inc.

McGovern, D. (2020). *The complete guide to competitive walking: Racewalking, power walking, Nordic walking, and more!* Locust Valley, NY: World Class Publications.

McGovern, D. (2016). *The complete guide to marathon walking*. Brattleboro, VT: Echo Point Books & Media.

O'Mara, S. (2019). *In praise of walking: A new scientific exploration*. New York: Penguin Random House.

Palomäki, J., Tammi, T., Lehtonen, N., Seittenranta, N., Laakasuo, M., Abuhamdeh, S., Lappi, O., & Cowley, B. U. (2021). The link between flow and performance is moderated by task experience. *Computers in Human Behavior, 124*(106891). https://doi.org/10.1016/j.chb.2021.106891.

Scott, L., & Stanten, M. (2020). *The walking solution: Get people walking for results*. Champaign, IL: Human Kinetics.

SECTION 4: EXPLORATION – And It's All Exploration

Kagge, E. (2020). *Walking: One step at a time*. New York: Vintage Books.

Nicholson, G. (2009). *The lost art of walking: The history, science, philosophy, and literature of pedestrianism*. New York: Riverhead Books.

Solnit, R. (2001). *Wanderlust: A history of walking*. New York: Penguin Books.

Speck, J. (2012). *Walkable city: How downtown can save America one step at a time*. New York: North Point Press.

Waters, Laura. (2019). *BeWILDered: Leaving everything behind for 3000km in the wilds of New Zealand*. South Melbourne, Victoria: Affirm Press.

"RITUALS ARE MAGICAL."
- ANDRÉ ACIMAN

To my granddaughter, Eloise. May walks of exhilaration and delight always be just outside your door.

All photos featured in the book are by Lee Scott, with some exceptions.*
Photo of Lee on page 33 taken by Madlen Reid.

*Cover: Shutterstock/Peshkova; pp.10–11: Shutterstock/Shawn.ccf; pp.28–29: Shutterstock/Andrew Mayovskyy; pp.64–67: Shutterstock/Zontica

Published in Canada by Plumleaf Press Inc. This is a first edition.

25 26 27 28 29   6 5 4 3 2 1

Library and Archives Canada Cataloguing in Publication
Title: Step outside : walking your way to health and happiness / by Lee Scott.
Names: Scott, Lee, 1969- author
Identifiers: Canadiana 20250185199 | ISBN 9781738165278 (softcover)
Subjects: LCSH: Fitness walking. | LCSH: Walking—Health aspects. | LCSH: Physical fitness.
Classification: LCC RA781.65 .S36 2025 | DDC 613.7/176—dc23

Publisher Cataloging-in-Publication Data (U.S.)
Names: Scott, Lee, 1969-, author.
Title: Step outside : walking your way to health and happiness /by Lee Scott. Description: Oakville, Ontario : Plumleaf Press, 2025, c2023. | Includes bibliographical references and index. | Summary: “The fitness leader and founder of WoW Power Walking shares decades of experience to help people find awe, fitness, and health from effective and accessible outdoor walking workouts”--Provided by publisher.
Identifiers: ISBN 978-1-73816-527-8 (paperback)
Subjects: LCSH: Physical fitness. | Fitness walking. | Walking. | Exercise. | BISAC: SPORTS & RECREATION / Walking. | SPORTS & RECREATION / Training.
Classification: LCC GV502.S34 2025| DDC 613.7/176 – dc23Original art created with

Designed by Alejandra León

Plumleaf Press Inc.
100 Bronte Road, Unit 9,
Oakville, ON, L6L 6L5

www.plumleafpress.com

Printed in China